D1409658

KAZUO ISHIGURO

My Twentieth Century Evening and Other Small Breakthroughs

THE NOBEL LECTURE

ALFRED A. KNOPF · NEW YORK · TORONTO · 2017

THIS IS A BORZOI BOOK PUBLISHED BY ALFRED A. KNOPF AND
ALFRED A. KNOPF CANADA

COPYRIGHT © 2017 BY THE NOBEL FOUNDATION

ALL RIGHTS RESERVED. PUBLISHED IN THE UNITED STATES BY
ALFRED A. KNOPF, A DIVISION OF PENGUIN RANDOM HOUSE LLC,
NEW YORK, AND IN CANADA BY ALFRED A. KNOPF CANADA,
A DIVISION OF PENGUIN RANDOM HOUSE CANADA
LIMITED, TORONTO.

WWW.AAKNOPF.COM
WWW.PENGUINRANDOMHOUSE.CA

KNOPF, BORZOI BOOKS, AND THE COLOPHON ARE REGISTERED
TRADEMARKS OF PENGUIN RANDOM HOUSE LLC. KNOPF CANADA
AND COLOPHON ARE TRADEMARKS OF PENGUIN RANDOM HOUSE
CANADA LIMITED.

THIS WORK IS A TRANSCRIPT OF THE NOBEL LECTURE IN
LITERATURE ORIGINALLY DELIVERED BY THE AUTHOR
AT THE SWEDISH ACADEMY IN STOCKHOLM, SWEDEN,
ON DECEMBER 7, 2017.

CATALOGING-IN-PUBLICATION DATA IS AVAILABLE AT THE
LIBRARY OF CONGRESS.
ISBN 9780525654957 (HARDCOVER)
ISBN 9780525654964 (EBOOK)

CATALOGING-IN-PUBLICATION DATA IS ON FILE AT THE
LIBRARY AND ARCHIVES CANADA
ISBN 9780735276130 (HARDCOVER)
ISBN 9780735276147 (EBOOK)

MANUFACTURED IN THE UNITED STATES OF AMERICA
FIRST EDITION

CASE DESIGN BY IRIS WEINSTEIN

The Nobel Prize in Literature 2017 was awarded to Kazuo Ishiguro "who, in novels of great emotional force, has uncovered the abyss beneath our illusory sense of connection with the world."

— THE SWEDISH ACADEMY

If you'd come across me in the autumn of 1979, you might have had some difficulty placing me, socially or even racially. I was then twenty-four years old. My features would have looked Japanese, but unlike most Japanese men seen in Britain in those days, I had hair down to my shoulders, and a drooping bandit-style moustache. The only accent discernible in my speech was that of someone brought up in the southern counties of England, inflected at times by the languid, already dated vernacular of the hippie era. If we'd got talking, we might have discussed the Total Footballers of Holland, or Bob Dylan's latest album, or perhaps the year I'd just spent working with homeless people in London. Had you mentioned Japan, asked me about its culture, you might even have detected a trace of impatience enter my manner as I declared my ignorance on the grounds that I hadn't set foot in that country—not even for a holiday—since leaving it at the age of five.

That autumn I'd arrived with a rucksack, a guitar and a portable typewriter in Buxton, Norfolk—a small English village with an old water mill and flat farm fields all around it. I'd come to this place because I'd been accepted on a one-year postgraduate Creative Writing course at the University of East Anglia. The university was ten miles away, in the cathedral town of Norwich, but I had no car and my only way of getting there was by means of a bus service that operated just once in the morning, once at lunchtime and once in the evening. But this, I was soon to discover, was no great

hardship: I was rarely required at the university more than twice a week. I'd rented a room in a small house owned by a man in his thirties whose wife had just left him. No doubt, for him, the house was filled with the ghosts of his wrecked dreams—or perhaps he just wanted to avoid me; in any case, I didn't set eyes on him for days on end. In other words, after the frenetic life I'd been leading in London, here I was, faced with an unusual amount of quiet and solitude in which to transform myself into a writer.

In fact, my little room was not unlike the classic writer's garret. The ceilings sloped claustrophobically—though if I stood on tiptoes I had a view, from my one window, of ploughed fields stretching away into the distance. There was a small table, the surface of which my typewriter and a desk lamp took up almost entirely. On the floor, instead of a bed, there was a large rectangular piece of industrial foam that would cause me to sweat in my sleep, even during the bitterly cold Norfolk nights.

It was in this room that I carefully examined the two short stories I'd written over the summer, wondering if they were good enough to submit to my new classmates. (We were, I knew, a class of six, meeting once every two weeks.) At that point in my life, I'd written little else of note in the way of prose fiction, having earned my place on the course with a radio play rejected by the BBC. In fact, having previously made firm plans to become a rock star by the time I was twenty, my literary ambitions had only recently made themselves known to me. The two stories I was now

scrutinising had been written in something of a panic, in response to the news that I'd been accepted on the university course. One was about a macabre suicide pact, the other about street fights in Scotland, where I'd spent some time as a community worker. They were not so good. I started another story, about an adolescent who poisons his cat, set like the others in present-day Britain. Then one night, during my third or fourth week in that little room, I found myself writing, with a new and urgent intensity, about Japan—about Nagasaki, the city of my birth, during the last days of the Second World War.

This, I should point out, came as something of a surprise to me. Today, the prevailing atmosphere is such that it's virtually an instinct for an aspiring young writer with a mixed cultural heritage to explore his "roots" in his work. But that was far from the case then. We were still a few years away from the explosion of "multicultural" literature in Britain. Salman Rushdie was an unknown with one out-of-print novel to his name. Asked to name the leading young British novelist of the day, people might have mentioned Margaret Drabble; of older writers, Iris Murdoch, Kingsley Amis, William Golding, Anthony Burgess, John Fowles. Foreigners like Gabriel García Márquez, Milan Kundera or Borges were read only in tiny numbers, their names meaningless even to keen readers.

Such was the literary climate of the day that when I finished that first Japanese story, for all my sense of having discovered an important new direction, I began immediately to wonder if this departure shouldn't be viewed as a self-indulgence; if I shouldn't quickly return to more "normal" subject matter. It was only after considerable hesitation that I began to show the story around, and I remain to this day profoundly grateful to my fellow students, to my tutors, Malcolm Bradbury and Angela Carter, and to the novelist Paul Bailey—that year the university's writer-in-residence—for their determinedly encouraging response. Had they been less positive, I would probably never again have written about Japan. As it was, I returned to my room and wrote and wrote. Throughout the winter of 1979–80, and well into the spring, I spoke to virtually no one aside from the other five students in my class, the village grocer from whom I bought the breakfast cereals and lamb kidneys on which I existed, and my girlfriend, Lorna (today my wife), who'd come to visit me every second weekend. It wasn't a balanced life, but in those four or five months I managed to complete one half of my first novel, *A Pale View of Hills*—set also in Nagasaki, in the years of recovery after the dropping of the atomic bomb. I can remember occasionally during this period tinkering with some ideas for short stories not set in Japan, only to find my interest waning rapidly.

Those months were crucial for me, in so far as without them I'd probably never have become a writer. Since then, I've often looked back and asked: What was going on with me? What was all this peculiar energy? My conclusion has been that just at that point in my life, I'd become engaged in an urgent act of preservation. To explain this, I'll need to go back a little.

•

I had come to England, aged five, with my parents and sister in April 1960, to the town of Guildford, Surrey, in the affluent "stockbroker belt" thirty miles south of London. My father was a research scientist, an oceanographer who'd come to work for the British government. The machine he went on to invent, incidentally, is today part of the permanent collection at the Science Museum in London.

The photographs taken shortly after our arrival show an England from a vanished era. Men wear woollen V-neck pullovers with ties, cars still have running boards and a spare wheel on the back. The Beatles, the sexual revolution, student protests, "multiculturalism" were all around the corner, but it's hard to believe the England our family first encountered even suspected it. To meet a foreigner from France or Italy was remarkable enough—never mind one from Japan.

Our family lived in a cul-de-sac of twelve houses just where the paved roads ended and the countryside began. It was less than a five-minute stroll to the local farm and the lane down which rows of cows trudged back and forth between fields. Milk was delivered by horse and cart. A common sight I remember vividly from my first days in England was that of hedgehogs—the cute, spiky, nocturnal creatures then numerous in that country—squashed by car wheels during the night, left in the morning dew, tucked neatly by the roadside, awaiting collection by the refuse men.

All our neighbours went to church, and when I went to play with their children, I noticed they said a small prayer before eating.

I attended Sunday school, and before long was singing in the church choir, becoming, aged ten, the first Japanese Head Chorister seen in Guildford. I went to the local primary school—where I was the only non-English child, quite possibly in the entire history of that school—and from when I was eleven, I travelled by train to my grammar school in a neighbouring town, sharing the carriage each morning with ranks of men in pinstripe suits and bowler hats, on their way to their offices in London.

By this stage, I'd become thoroughly trained in the manners expected of English middle-class boys in those days. When visiting a friend's house, I knew I should stand to attention the instant an adult wandered into the room; I learned that during a meal I had to ask permission before getting down from the table. As the only foreign boy in the neighbour-hood, a kind of local fame followed me around. Other children knew who I was before I met them. Adults who were total strangers to me sometimes addressed me by name in the street or in the local store.

When I look back to this period, and remember it was less than twenty years from the end of a world war in which the Japanese had been their bitter enemies, I'm amazed by the openness and instinctive generosity with which our family was accepted by this ordinary English community. The affection, respect and curiosity I retain to this day for that generation of Britons who came through the Second World War, and built a remarkable new welfare state in its aftermath, derive significantly from my personal experiences from those years.

But all this time, I was leading another life at home with my Japanese parents. At home there were different rules, different expectations, a different language. My parents' original intention had been that we return to Japan after a year, perhaps two. In fact, for our first eleven years in England, we were in a perpetual state of going back "next year." As a result, my parents' outlook remained that of visitors, not of immigrants. They'd often exchange observations about the curious customs of the natives without feeling any onus to adopt them. And for a long time the assumption remained that I would return to live my adult life in Japan, and efforts were made to keep up the Japanese side of my education. Each month a parcel arrived from Japan, containing the previous month's comics, magazines and educational digests, all of which I devoured eagerly. These parcels stopped arriving sometime in my teens—perhaps after my grandfather's death—but my parents' talk of old friends, relatives, episodes from their lives in Japan all kept up a steady supply of images and impressions. And then I always had my own store of memories—surprisingly vast and clear: of my grandparents, of favourite toys I'd left behind, the traditional Japanese house we'd lived in (which I can even today reconstruct in my mind room by room), my kindergarten, the local tram stop, the fierce dog that lived by the bridge, the chair in the barber's shop specially adapted for small boys, with a car steering wheel fixed in front of the big mirror.

What this all amounted to was that as I was growing up, long before I'd ever thought to

create fictional worlds in prose, I was busily constructing in my mind a richly detailed place called "Japan"—a place to which I in some way belonged, and from which I drew a certain sense of my identity and my confidence. The fact that I'd never physically returned to Japan during that time only served to make my own vision of the country more vivid and personal.

Hence the need for preservation. For by the time I reached my mid-twenties—though I never clearly articulated this at the time—I was coming to realise certain key things. I was starting to accept that "my" Japan perhaps didn't much correspond to any place I could go to on a plane; that the way of life of which my parents talked, that I remembered from my early childhood, had largely vanished during the 1960s and 1970s; that in any case, the Japan that existed in my head might always have been an emotional construct put together by a child out of memory, imagination and speculation. And perhaps most significantly, I'd come to realise that with each year I grew older, this Japan of mine—this precious place I'd grown up with—was getting fainter and fainter.

I'm now sure that it was this feeling, that "my" Japan was unique and at the same time terribly fragile—something not open to verification from outside—that drove me on to work in that small room in Norfolk. What I was doing was getting down on paper that world's special colours, mores, etiquettes; its dignity, its shortcomings, everything I'd ever thought about the place; before they faded forever from my mind. It was my wish to re-build my Japan in fiction, to make it safe, so that I could thereafter point to a book and say: "Yes, there's my Japan, inside there."

Spring 1983, three and a half years later. Lorna and I were now in London, lodging in two rooms at the top of a tall narrow house, which itself stood on a hill at one of the highest points of the city. There was a television mast nearby and when we tried to listen to records on our turntable, ghostly broadcasting voices would intermittently invade our speakers. Our living room had no sofa or armchair, but two mattresses on the floor covered with cushions. There was also a large table on which I wrote during the day, and where we had dinner at night. It wasn't luxurious, but we liked living there. I'd published my first novel the year before, and I'd also written a screenplay for a short film soon to be broadcast on British television.

I'd been for a time reasonably proud of my first novel, but by that spring, a niggling sense of dissatisfaction had set in. Here was the problem. My first novel and my first TV screenplay were too similar. Not in subject matter, but in method and style. The more I looked at it, the more my novel resembled a screenplay—dialogue plus directions. This was okay up to a point, but my wish now was to write fiction that could work properly *only on the page*. Why write a novel if it was going to offer more or less the same experience someone could get by turning on a television? How could written fiction hope to survive against the might of cinema and television if it didn't offer something unique, something the other forms couldn't do?

Around this time, I came down with a virus and spent a few days in bed. When I came out of the worst of it, and I didn't feel like sleeping all the time, I discovered that the heavy object, whose presence amidst my bedclothes had been annoying me for some time, was in fact a copy of the first volume of Marcel Proust's *Remembrance of Things Past* (as the title was then translated). There it was, so I started to read it. My still fevered condition was perhaps a factor, but I became completely riveted by the Overture and Combray sections. I read them over and over. Quite aside from the sheer beauty of these passages, I became thrilled by the means by which Proust got one episode to lead into the next. The ordering of events and scenes didn't follow the usual demands of chronology, nor those of a linear plot. Instead, tangential thought associations, or the vagaries of memory, seemed to move the writing from one episode to the next. Sometimes I found myself wondering: Why had these two seemingly unrelated moments been placed side by side in the narrator's mind? I could suddenly see an exciting, freer way of composing my second novel; one that could produce richness on the page and offer inner movements impossible to capture on any screen. If I could go from one passage to the next according to the narrator's thought associations and drifting memories, I could compose in something like the way an abstract painter might choose to place shapes and colours around a canvas. I could place a scene from two days ago right beside one from twenty years earlier, and ask the reader to ponder the relationship between the two. In such a way, I began to think, I might suggest the many layers of self-deception and denial that shrouded any person's view of their own self and of their past.

March 1988. I was thirty-three years old. We now had a sofa and I was lying across it, listening to a Tom Waits album. The previous year, Lorna and I had bought our own house in an unfashionable but pleasant part of South London, and in this house, for the first time, I had my own study. It was small, and didn't have a door, but I was thrilled to spread my papers around and not have to clear them away at the end of each day. And in that study—or so I believed—I'd just finished my third novel. It was my first not to have a Japanese setting—my personal Japan having been made less fragile by the writing of my previous novels. In fact my new book, to be called *The Remains of the Day,* seemed English in the extreme—though not, I hoped, in the manner of many British authors of the older generation. I'd been careful not to assume, as I felt many of them did, that my readers were all English, with native familiarity of English nuances and preoccupations. By then, writers like Salman Rushdie and V. S. Naipaul had forged the way for a more international, outward-looking British literature, one that didn't claim any centrality or automatic importance for Britain. Their writing was post-colonial in the widest sense. I wanted, like them, to write "international" fiction that could easily cross cultural and linguistic boundaries, even while writing a story set in what seemed a peculiarly English world. My version of England would be a kind of mythical one, whose outlines, I believed, were already present in the imaginations of many people around the world, including those who had never visited the country.

The story I'd just finished was about an English butler who realises, too late in his life, that he has lived his life by the wrong values; and that he's given his best years to serving a Nazi sympathiser; that by failing to take moral and political responsibility for his life, he has in some profound sense wasted that life. And more: that in his bid to become the perfect servant, he has forbidden himself to love, or be loved by, the one woman he cares for.

I'd read through my manuscript several times, and I'd been reasonably satisfied. Still, there was a niggling feeling that something was missing.

Then, as I say, there I was, in our house one evening, on our sofa, listening to Tom Waits. And Tom Waits began to sing a song called "Ruby's Arms." Perhaps some of you know it. (I even thought about singing it to you at this point, but I've changed my mind.) It's a ballad about a man, possibly a soldier, leaving his lover asleep in bed. It's the early morning, he goes down the road, gets on a train. Nothing unusual in that. But the song is delivered in the voice of a gruff American hobo utterly unaccustomed to revealing his deeper emotions.

And there comes a moment, midway through the song, when the singer tells us that his heart is breaking. The moment is almost unbearably moving because of the tension between the sentiment itself and the huge resistance that's obviously been overcome to declare it. Tom Waits sings the line with cathartic magnificence, and you feel a lifetime of tough-guy stoicism crumbling in the face of overwhelming sadness.

As I listened to Tom Waits, I realised what I'd still left to do. I'd unthinkingly made the decision, somewhere way back, that my English butler would maintain his emotional defences, that he'd manage to hide behind them, from himself and his reader, to the very end. Now I saw I had to reverse that decision. Just for one moment, towards the end of my story, a moment I'd have to choose carefully, I had to make his armour crack. I had to allow a vast and tragic yearning to be glimpsed underneath.

I should say here that I have, on a number of other occasions, learned crucial lessons from the voices of singers. I refer here less to the lyrics being sung, and more to the actual singing. As we know, a human voice in song is capable of expressing an unfathomably complex blend of feelings. Over the years, specific aspects of my writing have been influenced by, among others, Bob Dylan, Nina Simone, Emmylou Harris, Ray Charles, Bruce Springsteen, Gillian Welch and my friend and collaborator Stacey Kent. Catching something in their voices, I've said to myself: "Ah yes, that's it. That's what I need to capture in that scene. Something very close to that." Often it's an emotion I can't quite put into words, but there it is, in the singer's voice, and now I've been given something to aim for.

In October 1999, I was invited by the German poet Christoph Heubner on behalf of the International Auschwitz Committee to spend a few days visiting the former concentration camp. My accommodation was at the Auschwitz Youth Meeting Centre on the road between the first Auschwitz camp and the Birkenau death camp two miles away. I was shown around these sites and met, informally, three survivors. I felt I'd come close, geographically at least, to the heart of the dark force under whose shadow my generation had grown up. At Birkenau, on a wet afternoon, I stood before the rubbled remains of the gas chambers—now strangely neglected and unattended—left much as the Germans had left them after blowing them up and fleeing the Red Army. They were now just damp, broken slabs, exposed to the harsh Polish climate, deteriorating year by year. My hosts talked about their dilemma. Should these remains be protected? Should Perspex domes be built to cover them over, to preserve them for the eyes of succeeding generations? Or should they be allowed, slowly and naturally, to rot away to nothing? It seemed to me a powerful metaphor for a larger dilemma. How were such memories to be preserved? Would the glass domes transform these relics of evil and suffering into tame museum exhibits? What should we choose to remember? When is it better to forget and move on?

I was forty-four years old. Until then I'd considered the Second World War, its horrors and its triumphs, as belonging to my parents' generation. But now it occurred to me that before too long, many who had witnessed those huge events at first hand would not be alive. And what then? Did the burden of remembering fall to my own generation? We hadn't experienced the war years, but we'd at least been brought up by parents whose lives had been indelibly shaped by them. Did I, now, as a public teller of stories, have a duty I'd hitherto been unaware of? A duty to pass on, as best I could, these memories and lessons from our parents' generation to the one after our own?

A little while later, I was speaking before an audience in Tokyo, and a questioner from the floor asked, as is common, what I might work on next. More specifically, the questioner pointed out that my books had often concerned individuals who'd lived through times of great social and political upheaval, and who then looked back over their lives and struggled to come to terms with their darker, more shameful memories. Would my future books, she asked, continue to cover a similar territory?

I found myself giving a quite unprepared answer. Yes, I said, I'd often written about such individuals struggling between forgetting and remembering. But in the future, what I really wished to do was to write a story about how a nation or a community faced these same questions. Does a nation remember and forget in much the same way as an individual does? Or are there important differences? What exactly are the memories of a nation? Where are they kept? How are they shaped and controlled?

Are there times when forgetting is the only way to stop cycles of violence, or to stop a society disintegrating into chaos or war? On the other hand, can stable, free nations really be built on foundations of wilful amnesia and frustrated justice? I heard myself telling the questioner that I wanted to find a way to write about these things, but that for the moment, unfortunately, I couldn't think how I'd do it.

One evening in early 2001, in the darkened front room of our house in North London (where we were by then living), Lorna and I began to watch, on a reasonable quality VHS tape, a 1934 Howard Hawks film called *Twentieth Century*. The film's title, we soon discovered, referred not to the century we'd then just left behind but to a famous luxury train of the era connecting New York and Chicago. As some of you will know, the film is a fast-paced comedy, set largely on the train, concerning a Broadway producer who, with increasing desperation, tries to prevent his leading actress going to Hollywood to become a movie star. The film is built around a huge comic performance by John Barrymore, one of the great actors of his day. His facial expressions, his gestures, almost every line he utters come layered with ironies, contradictions, the grotesqueries of a man drowning in egocentricity and self-dramatisation. It is in many ways a brilliant performance. Yet, as the film continued to unfold, I found myself curiously uninvolved. This puzzled me at first. I usually liked Barrymore, and was a big enthusiast for Howard

Hawks's other films from this period—such as *His Girl Friday* and *Only Angels Have Wings*. Then, around the film's one-hour mark, a simple, striking idea came into my head. The reason why so many vivid, undeniably convincing characters in novels, films and plays so often failed to touch me was because these characters didn't connect to any of the other characters in an interesting human relationship. And immediately, this next thought came regarding my own work: What if I stopped worrying about my characters and worried instead about my relationships?

As the train rattled farther west and John Barrymore became ever more hysterical, I thought about E. M. Forster's famous distinction between three-dimensional and two-dimensional characters. A character in a story became three-dimensional, he'd said, by virtue of the fact that they "surprised us convincingly." It was in so doing they became "rounded." But what, I now wondered, if a character was three-dimensional, while all his or her relationships were not? Elsewhere in that same lecture series, Forster had used a humorous image, of extracting the storyline out of a novel with a pair of forceps and holding it up, like a wriggling worm, for examination under the light. Couldn't I perform a similar exercise and hold up to the light the various relationships that crisscross any story? Could I do this with my own work—to stories I'd completed and ones I was planning? I could look at, say, this mentor-pupil relationship. Does it say something insightful and fresh? Or now that I was staring at it, does it become obvious it's a tired stereotype, identical to those found in hundreds of mediocre stories? Or this relationship between two competitive friends: Is it dynamic? Does it have emotional resonance? Does it evolve? Does it surprise convincingly? Is it three-dimensional? I suddenly felt I understood better why in the past various aspects of my work had failed, despite my applying desperate remedies. The thought came to me—as I continued to stare at John Barrymore—that all good stories, never mind how radical or traditional their mode of telling, had to contain relationships that are important to us; that move us, amuse us, anger us, surprise us. Perhaps in future, if I attended more to my relationships, my characters would take care of themselves.

It occurs to me as I say this that I might be making a point here that has always been plainly obvious to you. But all I can say is that it was an idea that came to me surprisingly late in my writing life, and I see it now as a turning point, comparable with the others I've been describing to you today. From then on, I began to build my stories in a different way. When writing my novel *Never Let Me Go,* for instance, I set off from the start by thinking about its central relationships triangle, and then the other relationships that fanned out from it.

Important turning points in a writer's career—perhaps in many kinds of career—are like these. Often, they are small, scruffy moments. They are quiet, private sparks of revelation. They don't come often, and when they do, they may well come without fanfare, unendorsed by mentors or colleagues. They must often compete for attention with louder, seemingly more urgent demands. Sometimes what they reveal may go against the grain of prevailing wisdom. But when they come, it's important to be able to recognise them for what they are. Or they'll slip through your hands.

I've been emphasising here the small and the private, because essentially that's what my work is about. One person writing in a quiet room, trying to connect with another person, reading in another quiet—or maybe not so quiet—room. Stories can entertain, sometimes teach or argue a point. But for me the essential thing is that they communicate feelings. That they appeal to what we share as human beings across our borders and divides. There are large glamorous industries around stories; the book industry, the movie industry, the television industry, the theatre industry. But in the end, stories are about one person saying to another: This is the way it feels to me. Can you understand what I'm saying? Does it also feel this way to you?

So we come to the present. I woke up recently to the realisation I'd been living for some years in a bubble. That I'd failed to notice the frustration and anxieties of many people around me. I saw that my world—a civilised, stimulating place filled with ironic, liberal-minded people—was in fact much smaller than I'd ever imagined. 2016, a year of surprising—and for me depressing—political events in Europe and in America, and of sickening acts of terrorism all around the globe, forced me to acknowledge that the unstoppable advance of liberal-humanist values I'd taken for granted since childhood may have been an illusion.

I'm part of a generation inclined to optimism, and why not? We watched our elders successfully transform Europe from a place of totalitarian regimes, genocide and historically unprecedented carnage to a much-envied region of liberal democracies living in near-borderless friendship. We watched the old colonial empires crumble around the world together with the reprehensible assumptions that underpinned them. We saw significant progress in feminism, gay rights and the battles on several fronts against racism. We grew up against a backdrop of the great clash—ideological and military—between capitalism and communism, and witnessed what many of us believed to be a happy conclusion.

But now, looking back, the era since the fall of the Berlin Wall seems like one of complacency, of opportunities lost. Enormous inequalities—of wealth and opportunity—have been allowed to grow, between nations and within nations. In particular, the disastrous invasion of Iraq in 2003, and the long years of austerity policies imposed on ordinary people following the scandalous economic crash of 2008, have brought us to a present in which Far Right ideologies and tribal nationalisms proliferate. Racism, in its traditional forms and in its modernised, better-marketed versions, is once again on the rise, stirring beneath our civilised streets like a buried monster awakening. For the moment we seem to lack any progressive cause to unite us. Instead, even in the wealthy democracies of the West, we're fracturing into rival camps from which to compete bitterly for resources or power.

And around the corner—or have we already turned this corner?—lie the challenges posed by stunning breakthroughs in science, technology and medicine. New genetic technologies—such as the gene-editing technique CRISPR—and advances in Artificial Intelligence and robotics will bring us amazing, lifesaving benefits, but may also create savage meritocracies that resemble apartheid, and massive unemployment, including to those in the current professional elites.

So here I am, a man in my sixties, rubbing

my eyes and trying to discern the outlines, out there in the mist, to this world I didn't suspect even existed until yesterday. Can I, a tired author, from an intellectually tired generation, now find the energy to look at this unfamiliar place? Do I have something left that might help to provide perspective, to bring emotional layers to the arguments, fights and wars that will come as societies struggle to adjust to huge changes?

I'll have to carry on and do the best I can. Because I still believe that literature is important, and will be particularly so as we cross this difficult terrain. But I'll be looking to the writers from the younger generations to inspire and lead us. This is their era, and they will have the knowledge and instinct about it that I will lack. In the worlds of books, cinema, TV and theatre I see today adventurous, exciting talents: women and men in their forties, thirties and twenties. So I am optimistic. Why shouldn't I be?

But let me finish by making an appeal—if you like, my Nobel appeal! It's hard to put the whole world to rights, but let us at least think about how we can prepare our own small corner of it, this corner of "literature," where we read, write, publish, recommend, denounce and give awards to books. If we are to play an important role in this uncertain future, if we are to get the best from the writers of today and tomorrow, I believe we must become more diverse. I mean this in two particular senses.

Firstly, we must widen our common literary world to include many more voices from beyond our comfort zones of the elite first-world cultures. We must search more energetically to discover the gems from what remain today unknown literary cultures, whether the writers live in faraway countries or within our own communities. Second, we must take great care not to set too narrowly or conservatively our definitions of what constitutes good literature. The next generation will come with all sorts of new, sometimes bewildering ways to tell important and wonderful stories. We must keep our minds open to them, especially regarding genre and form, so that we can nurture and celebrate the best of them. In a time of dangerously increasing division, we must listen. Good writing and good reading will break down barriers. We may even find a new idea, a great humane vision, around which to rally.

To the Swedish Academy, the Nobel Foundation and to the people of Sweden who down the years have made the Nobel Prize a shining symbol for the good we human beings strive for—I give my thanks.

THE WORKS OF KAZUO ISHIGURO

A Pale View of Hills

An Artist of the Floating World

The Remains of the Day

The Unconsoled

When We Were Orphans

Never Let Me Go

Nocturnes

The Buried Giant

Kazuo Ishiguro was born in Nagasaki, Japan, in 1954 and moved to Britain at the age of five. His eight works of fiction have earned him many awards and honors around the world, including the Nobel Prize in Literature and the Booker Prize. His work has been translated into more than fifty languages. *The Remains of the Day* and *Never Let Me Go* were made into acclaimed films. Ishiguro also writes screenplays and song lyrics. He lives in London with his wife and daughter.

A NOTE ON THE TYPE

This book was set in Granjon, a type named in compliment to Robert Granjon, a type cutter and printer active in Antwerp, Lyons, Rome, and Paris from 1523 to 1590. Granjon, the boldest and most original designer of his time, was one of the first to practice the trade of typefounder apart from that of printer.

Composed by North Market Street Graphics,
Lancaster, Pennsylvania

Printed and bound by Thomson-Shore,
Dexter, Michigan

Designed by Iris Weinstein